the
near
surround

the
near
surround

nancy mitchell

four way books
new york

Editorial Office
Four Way Books
PO Box 535, Village Station
New York, NY 10014
www.fourwaybooks.com

Library of Congress
Catalog Card Number: 2001 132489

ISBN 1-884800-42-4

Cover Art: Wendy Goldberg
Book Design: Brunel

This book is manufactured in the United States of America and
printed on acid-free paper.

Four Way Books is a division of Friends of Writers, Inc.,
a Vermont-based not-for-profit organization. We are grateful
for the assistance we receive from individual donors and
private foundations.

ACKNOWLEDGMENTS

Thanks to the editors of the following magazines in which these poems originally appeared, some in different versions.

Agni	What about
	Dropped Thing
The Marlboro Review	As Told by the Mother
Louisville Review	Love Story in Subtitles
North Atlantic Review	Animals Who Have Known Me
Salt Hill Journal	The Leaving
Last Call	Love Story in Subtitles
edited by Sarah Gorham	Runaway
and Jeffrey Skinner	The Leaving
Sarabande Books, 1997	Incognito
	Today I conjure your spirit
	(as "Progress")

The epigraph is from *The Selected Poetry of Rainer Maria Rilke*, edited and translated by Stephen Mitchell, published by Random House.

Thank you to Martha Rhodes and Dzvinia Orlowsky for their deep and intuitive responses to the manuscript as well as their meticulous editing suggestions. Thanks to the following writers for their generous responses and encouragement: Bob Svenson, George Kalamaras, Terri Ford, Steve Huff, and Michael Burkard. Thanks to Debbie Gichner, Cathy Miller, Gary Harrington, Mihaela Moscaliuc, Kelly Rouse, and Deb Merkle for their sustaining support. Thanks to Beth Holchholzer for her unstinting hospitality, and to the Virginia Center for the Creative Arts for a residency fellowship.

For John,
Zachary, Sara, and Seth

CONTENTS

I

II

III

IV

What seems so far from you is most your own

—Rainer Maria Rilke
The Sonnets to Orpheus

I

What about

sushi with the Merkles
merlot or cabernet would be fine with Martin

What about
taking Max for a stroll at sunset
taking Max

What about
dinner with the dean
coffee with Don at ten

What about
he said he'd call by 11
hopping in the shower at 11:15
dropping the whole thing

What about
she doesn't like to be on top

What about
mayonnaise method
of removing water stain
from wood

What about
Mother's face
behind
a comic book

Brother's face

What about
        lime neon bra
        with matching panties

        a doll with my face

        a full-time phone lover
        a phone life
        a phone liar
        a phony

        the silence of cold spoons

Awakened as a Child

Swarms of stamp-sized
baby Christs, each halo
aglow with Byzantine gold.

I worried if what I'd seen

was a blessing or curse—
from the wall the iridescent crucifix
gleamed equivocally green.

Morning, not a speck of gold
dust. I buried that crucifix
next to the grave of my dog Sheba.

Runaway

A block from her mother's house
in a wooded lot where all summer

men in cherry pickers unwittingly
graced her grave with wisteria

cut clear from power lines:
the hole they dug her from,

the shoveled piles of dirt
studded with small red flags.

Dropped Thing

Dropped by someone
alone in a low boat?

Low boat so far out
can't be seen.

Dropped down water
like a feather through air,

dropped unintentionally
or intentionally slipped.

Falls Church Condo

How to go back
for the drop-leaf

table left behind
and the white pine

bureau. How to
return to where

pull the knob—
the closet door falls down.

For Years I Hid Things from Myself

The heart
on its chain,

I think, buried
in the yard

(when I'd lie on my back
the heart would lie

in the hollow
of my collarbone).

To the underside
of a bed, a table, I nailed

a tarot deck, an undershirt,
a faceless plastic saint—

to stop looking at them,
to breathe.

My blood

the color of merlot

from vein to vial
air doesn't have a chance

to mix with it.

At every paint store
they said *Sorry,*

we don't carry much
in this line of red.

Love Story in Subtitles

It won't be long before he replaces her.
I'm glad she has taken the dog.

As Told by the Mother

Light rain the daughter remembers
becomes torrential.

Small shopping trip—
a quest; the few stores

all the stalls in noisy
bazaar of old Istanbul.

A horse drawn carriage.

At last found (after hope was lost
and horses hung wet, weary heads):

pink ballet slippers: soft
to the daughter's touch

as skin on her foot,
far too fragile for dancing.

The First Return

You see your face
among the masks
your mother made
and hung in the room
where you sleep.

They guard your dreams—
you know better; you've seen her
behind her studio screen
whisper into the clay, shape
their eyes with spit.

You're smart to keep
dreams to yourself;
a sly one like her
would know a kind ear
is the first way in.

What You <u>Did</u> Say

Maybe I could paint.

Did <u>not</u> say: *Is this all*
you brought me from France:
an Eiffel Tower key chain?

<u>Did</u> say as I stumbled,
you leaning on me to walk:
Remember, my hips are glass.

Got a light? propped against
the butcher block, blowing smoke
toward the door: *I don't want*
anyone to come here.

Your radiance the day
of your last breath . . .

Oh yeah, right,—
you would've laughed.

The way the light lay

white across the hospital sheet
becomes a motif.

Yellow roses will insinuate
into symbol,

as will the peripheral smell
of sterilizing gel,

the respirator's
shuddering down.

A light fog stalls on the bay
bridge to your house:

porcelain bobby pin dish,
silk rose robe clinging

to your bathroom door hook,
faded lipsticked cigarettes

lying in a field of ash.
Your small scrawl all

across October, your voice
still on the answering machine

you have reached

Your Drawing

I'm ashamed
to return

the small pencil
drawing; I damaged it
first by folding,

then by trying to steam
and iron out the fold.

Seedlings

In the dark
on our knees

your hands
on my hands

we mound dirt
around each

The Whole Bottle

My mother would never
have discussed it,

she was reserved—*for whom?*—

this same reserve in me
a locked vault door,

the key a hieroglyph
lost in childhood—

but whose . . . hers? mine?

I held her the way I never could

but wished I could have
before she died,

before this dream
I'm just waking up from

of my holding her
in my brother's old

back bedroom, lying on his bed,
hearing the whoever

drag the whatever
across the attic floor.

Held her like I've held
my children,

folded her in my arms,
brought the blanket

up all around her,
tucked the strands

of hair behind her ear,
kissed her skin,

so thin against my lips
and her forehead.

Dark Dream

Two cats running between my legs,
then the *Be still* voice,

and it's black-dark and I'm still.
More cats and they're making me choose.

The place I go is where I go
to lie on the stainless steel table.

I want to grab the nurse's hand—
practice, practice, practice falling.

Don't Call It Anything

Don't fill it in just to fill it in.

I'm not speaking to anyone until five.
Let's see how sick you get of it.

Childhood Koan:
  You don't get to go back.
  You can only work with what you've got.
  Everything must take up the same space proportionately.

Don't look at them look at you.
Don't look at them, look at you.

I'm doing more with my left hand.

Toward a more perfect moon;
wave practicing wave.

You know she lived nine years in Egypt.
Egypt: land of the Dad.

New England Salt Box
Windsor Chair.

Isosceles:
Your face, ten years later.

II

Possible You

I run past you, interesting, I think,
but am put off by the tiny, black,
groomed-to-a-tee poodle. I like your beard
but then again, there's the poodle. Your nose
is big, but you wear your beret with an aplomb
rarely seen in this country. Far down
the beach I run away from you. You're still
with that poodle on the boardwalk bench
when I walk back. Lying on the sand in front of you
I watch the sea. I turn my face to the sun
then away. Are you both still there?

Drought, Stonedust

Don't know if we can
save newly laid sod—

nineteen days without rain,
the way we beat it down

rolling loaded wheelbarrows
over and over and over

from stonedust hill
to fill the path snaking

our garden—bird bath
auspiciously placed, red

dragon guarding moonflower—
rusty dry patches like scrapes

on the knees of the child
whose hand we let go one split second.

*With what we're paying to water
we could have gone to Greece—*

rooms noon-shuttered
against the high white sun.

Late Fall and Still No Hard Frost

And still the leaves cling
to these trees like old brown bats . . .

He wishes she wouldn't make
such macabre connections
(she is so lonely in this new city),

he wants there to be just one bare tree,
its fucking leaves finally fallen.

For how long

did you look before
you could see the shadows

in the water glass
were an entire city,

each building
lifted by the light?

Two-Faced Moon

Or, as some have said, doubled
in water, but I didn't and still don't
because this is how I was seeing it:

the one face in the sky, cut
by branches, and the other on the pond,
somehow more whole and swimming.

I might not have called it two-faced
before you turned your other face to me,
but, after I began to see it that way,

I began to think that it was, after all, OK,
that everything has at least two faces:

night sky, branches, water, and doesn't-matter.

The Chosen

Called forth by you
years ago through
the long tunnel

you made by holding
a mirror to a mirror.

You will see me again—
disguised as a gardener,
picking bees from my sack

to feed birds
that live on low branches.

Animals Who Have Known Me

The lame, walleyed and ailing.
The flea-bitten and ringwormed, bellies
swaying with tiers of teat—strengthened
by meat my mother pilfered from my father's plate—
I named them all after her.

The lies I whispered into their ears:
You are the toughest dog
in all of Morehead City,
or, *the fiercest of cats.*

When I see some of them
between alleys, I call *Marie, Marie*
but they turn their heads away,
or look me straight in the eye
as if they never knew me.

III

Truce

No guns, but no breeze.
No fists and bricks, but no birds.

It's going to be dark.
It's going to be black and white.

All Winter I Keep to Myself

Twin star,
twin water,
you leave me
to survive:
three I-Ching coins,
the sea at night,

and this pen
to worry my life along.

Incognito

In the middle of night, wet
and trembling from so near
a drown,
I arrive shipwrecked
at your door.

You ask me to come in,
liking things lost, then found.

You warm my feet,
lick salt from each toe.

Still you don't know it's me.

Bed and Breakfast

We turn down the four-poster bed to sheets
the same ivied pattern as at home. Pink pin-striped
wallpaper discreetly hides the cracked plaster.

A couple of dead-beat angels
supervise from the mantel.

Regret all the way down the wide staircase
to breakfast on the wrap-around porch:
the years lost, the children never imagined.

About the Child

It's not true
what I told you
about not grieving.

I banished it
to another room
another house
in another country

The Last One

Comforter thrown back
over and over, books

flung from the bed
thudding the floor,

muttering down the hall:
this is the last one.

Waking up alone

I thought for a minute
making love with you

must have been a piece
of the dream:

small stars falling
to the ground

Tuesday Morning

Her breath fogs the window,
the window clears,

fogs the window,
it clears again.

Far Edge

Where she had peed in the dirt,
five years later

he put his hands in the same dirt,
tasted it and wept.

Who is he who could do such?
Who is she that he would do such?

Mornings, Ever Since

Same noisy, dingy scatter
of sparrows from the hedgerow
ghetto mine the blue dawn
moonscape of week-old snow.

Another night of still
not sleeping, up to make
tea in the kitchen dark:
hot tap water full blast

into the cast iron kettle
slammed on the wreath
of blue-white flame.

Every Last Plate

I think I'll smash a few for you.
Because you're sitting there. In that chair.

Watching me like a seismologist.
Then I'll sling a stack or two for my father

who left our house without a photo of any of us,
who never showed up for a single school play

or baseball game . . . or, did, drunk
and yelling, *Stupid, just hit the ball.*

The Near Surround

Far edge,
afternoon field

a shape suggests itself
but not enough to begin

the long journey for:
too many times the cypress

beyond the lane's curve
was your hooded posture,

your shadow darkened
the white lawn chair.

Now I watch
what gathers between us,

between me
and what isn't you.

The Sea Tamped Flat with Gray

Turn from the sea, walk that long block
to the bookstore of his indifference—

frenetic with fluorescence and flyers,
metallic coffee, the chairs folding-prayer-meeting.

Given

Why did I sit with my back
to the sea? Although
the glare of the sun
was a good excuse.

To make up
for the storm the day before,
the embarrassment of very bad food,
bees haunting the butter
and the stainless steel creamer.

I made a long list
of things I would give you,
starting with my back.

Syntactically Correct

I saw your list of possibilities:
readings, places to publish, new haircut,
and ATM pin number;
short list falling from the counter
among other papers falling.

Certain each will *pan out,*
like the extravagant lie
that you had just mailed the key
to your back door,
how *all the metal detectors
in the post offices between Boston
and Albany will be going crazy,*
then, put the key in my hand
right before you knew I'd break
it off. Syntactically correct,
heartfelt: blotto.

Souvenir

That thin brown book:
I want it back.

Your army picture
is stuck in it, black phone
to your ear, fronting the flag.

The book looked like dirt,
smelled like dirt too.
I held it with both hands.

I watched you so carefully
hide it in the duffel bag
you walked out with.

Message via Our Mutual Friend

Could I possibly send the things
you, in a hurry to leave, left behind?

You mean the green cat-eye marble
you rolled between my breasts,
the sweater still smelling of sweat
and cigarette smoke, the small plastic
donkey that brayed *Believe*
into the early days of your sobriety?

All in a very dark closet
until you ask for them yourself.

Until then your mother remains tired—
standing with your father in the photo
taken on their porch . . . she wants to sit down.
Your father is impatient . . . and the grass,
the grass has been growing all this time.

The Leaving

To steady me,
to keep me from rising—

that last night with him, lying down,
he placed his hand on the space
where my ribs furl back like wings

to steady me,
to keep me from rising.

IV

Hereafter

Straighten the lamp shade
and the whole house steadies.

All the people in my life,
just who they should be.

Sunsets routinely spectacular
and each turned page whispers *Yes.*

Today I conjure your spirit

where before it came
on its own; this is a good sign.

Your letters—taken
from the nightstand

stuffed in the dark
basement cupboard—

no longer among the first
things I will save

from fire. And if a small
memory of you should arrive

it will be like the shadow
against these white blinds:

a bird, a leaf
or some other bird.

Town-Side of Sea Run

Right turn on Atlantic Ave., past
the house with the always-hard-
for-me-to-pronounce *trompe l'oeil*—
a parrot in a palm,

up to the two miles of boardwalk, strict
geometry of pilings and plank,
chalkboard of sky
intermittently and cryptically inscribed

by a bird
or a flock of them, a herd of clouds
or one

or none,

and that sun,
into which I'm running.

Nancy Mitchell received an MFA from the Warren Wilson MFA Program for Writers in 1991. She teaches in the English Department and Honors Program at Salisbury University, and is guest lecturer for Delmarva Discussions on the Eastern Shore of Maryland, Delaware and Virginia. She has received grants from the Artist in the Schools Programs in Arlington, Virginia and a residency fellowship from the Virginia Center for the Creative Arts, Sweetbrier, Virginia. Her poems have appeared in *Agni, The Marlboro Review, Salt Hill Journal, Louisville Review, North Atlantic Review, Last Call* (an anthology published by Sarabande Books) and on the website *Poetry Daily*. She lives in Salisbury, Maryland.